How To Stop Intrusive Thoughts

:

The Nature Of The Human Mind Reset, How To Use CBT To Overcome Negative Self-Talk, Cognitive Distortion, Obsessive Compulsive Disorder, And Toxic Thoughts To Gain Mental Freedom.

Introduction

Have you ever found yourself trapped in a relentless cycle of negative thoughts that seem to invade your mind, no matter how hard you try to push them away? Have you ever felt overwhelmed by feelings of anxiety, self-doubt, or guilt, unable to escape the grip of your own mind? If so, you're not alone. Intrusive thoughts are a common experience for many people, but they need not dictate the course of our lives. In this book, we will explore the nature of intrusive thoughts and how they can be overcome through the transformative power of Cognitive Behavioral Therapy (CBT).

What is it about the human mind that makes it susceptible to intrusive thoughts? Why do we sometimes find ourselves stuck in patterns of negative self-talk and rumination, unable to break free from the cycle of our own thoughts? These are questions that have puzzled philosophers, psychologists, and neuroscientists for centuries. But through the lens of CBT, we can begin to unravel the mysteries of the human mind and gain a deeper understanding of how our thoughts, emotions, and behaviors are interconnected.

Negative self-talk, cognitive distortion, obsessive-compulsive disorder (OCD), and toxic thoughts are all manifestations of the complex workings of the human mind. But they are not insurmountable obstacles. By employing the principles of CBT, we can learn to challenge and reframe our negative thoughts, break free from the grip of cognitive distortions, and overcome the compulsions that fuel our obsessions. In doing so, we can gain mental freedom and reclaim control over our own minds.

But what exactly is CBT, and how does it work? How can we use CBT techniques to overcome intrusive thoughts and gain mental freedom? These are questions that we will explore in depth throughout this book. We will delve into the underlying principles of CBT, examine the common types of intrusive thoughts, and discuss how CBT can be applied to manage a range of mental health conditions, from anxiety and depression to OCD and beyond.

Moreover, we will explore the role of mindfulness and self-compassion in the CBT process, and discuss strategies for identifying and challenging negative self-talk and cognitive distortions. Through engaging questions and practical exercises, readers will be guided on a journey of self-discovery and transformation, learning how to cultivate greater awareness, resilience, and well-being in their own lives.

Ultimately, the goal of this book is to empower readers to take control of their own mental health and find freedom from the tyranny of intrusive thoughts. It is a journey of self-discovery and self-empowerment, guided by the principles of CBT and fueled by the courage and determination of the human spirit. So if you're ready to embark on this journey towards mental freedom, then let's begin. Together, we will explore the depths of the human mind and discover the power that lies within each and

every one of us to overcome intrusive thoughts
and live a life of greater peace, clarity, and joy.

Table Of Contents

Chapter 1: Understanding Intrusive Thoughts
- Defining intrusive thoughts
- Exploring the common types of intrusive thoughts
- Recognizing the impact of intrusive thoughts on mental well-being

Chapter 2: The Nature of the Human Mind
- Examining the workings of the human mind
- Understanding the mechanisms behind intrusive thoughts
- Discussing the relationship between thoughts, emotions, and behaviors

Chapter 3: Introduction to Cognitive Behavioral Therapy (CBT)
- Explaining the principles of CBT
- Understanding how CBT can be applied to manage intrusive thoughts
- Discussing the effectiveness of CBT in treating various mental health conditions

Chapter 4: Identifying Negative Self-Talk
- Recognizing patterns of negative self-talk
- Exploring the origins of negative beliefs and attitudes
- Learning to challenge and reframe negative self-talk using CBT techniques

Chapter 5: Understanding Cognitive Distortions
- Defining cognitive distortions
- Identifying common cognitive distortions associated with intrusive thoughts
- Learning strategies to counter cognitive distortions through CBT

Chapter 6: Overcoming Obsessive-Compulsive Disorder (OCD)
- Understanding the nature of OCD
- Exploring the role of intrusive thoughts in OCD
- Introducing CBT techniques specifically tailored for managing OCD symptoms

Chapter 7: Managing Toxic Thoughts
- Recognizing toxic thoughts and their impact on mental health
- Learning strategies to identify and challenge toxic thoughts using CBT
- Exploring mindfulness techniques to promote mental clarity and emotional resilience

Chapter 8: Practicing Mindfulness and Self-Compassion
- Introducing mindfulness as a tool for managing intrusive thoughts
- Cultivating self-compassion to counteract self-criticism and judgment
- Incorporating mindfulness and self-compassion practices into daily life

Chapter 9: Sustaining Progress and Moving Forward
- Reflecting on the journey of overcoming intrusive thoughts
- Developing strategies to maintain progress and prevent relapse
- Setting goals for continued personal growth and well-being

Conclusion: Embracing Mental Freedom
- Encouraging readers to continue applying CBT techniques to achieve mental freedom
- Inspiring hope and resilience in the journey toward overcoming intrusive thoughts

Chapter 1: Understanding Intrusive Thoughts

- Defining intrusive thoughts
- Exploring the common types of intrusive thoughts
- Recognizing the impact of intrusive thoughts on mental well-being

Defining intrusive thoughts

Intrusive thoughts are a manifestation of the complexities inherent in the human psyche, representing a phenomenon characterized by the unwelcome intrusion of distressing, irrational, or disturbing thoughts into one's consciousness. These thoughts often emerge suddenly and involuntarily, disrupting the tranquility of one's inner world with their persistent and intrusive nature. Unlike passing whims or fleeting daydreams, intrusive thoughts possess a tenacious grip on the mind, compelling individuals to confront unsettling scenarios or distressing imagery against their will.

These intrusive thoughts possess a cunning ability to disguise themselves as our own, blending seamlessly with the fabric of our inner dialogue. They may take the form of worries about the future, regrets about the past, or disturbing images that seem to materialize out of nowhere. With every unwelcome intrusion, they cast shadows over our sense of peace and well-being, leaving behind a residue of anxiety and discomfort.

Like relentless adversaries, intrusive thoughts often defy logic and reason, persisting even in the face of evidence to the contrary. They thrive on uncertainty, feeding off our doubts and insecurities like parasites clinging to a host. Despite our best efforts to banish them, they linger like stubborn echoes, echoing their disquieting refrains in the chambers of our consciousness.

At their core, intrusive thoughts are often rooted in anxiety, fear, or unresolved psychological conflicts, manifesting as recurring themes or scenarios that evoke feelings of discomfort or distress. They may take various forms, ranging from fleeting doubts or worries to vivid and disturbing mental images that provoke intense emotional reactions. Despite their subjective nature, intrusive thoughts can exert a profound impact on an individual's mental well-being, contributing to feelings of unease, guilt, or shame.

One of the defining characteristics of intrusive thoughts is their persistence and resistance to rationalization or dismissal. Unlike passing thoughts that can be easily brushed aside, intrusive thoughts tend to linger, intruding upon the consciousness with relentless insistence. Despite efforts to suppress or ignore them, these thoughts persist like stubborn echoes, perpetuating a cycle of rumination and distress that can erode one's sense of peace and stability.

Moreover, intrusive thoughts often possess a quality of irrationality or improbability that sets them apart from ordinary concerns or worries. They may involve scenarios that defy logic or contradict one's core values and beliefs, causing individuals to question the integrity of their own thought processes. In this sense, intrusive thoughts represent a disruption of the cognitive filtering mechanisms that typically govern the flow of information within the mind, leading to a sense of cognitive dissonance and internal conflict.

While intrusive thoughts are a common experience for many individuals, they can become particularly distressing or debilitating when they escalate into more severe forms of psychopathology, such as obsessive-compulsive disorder (OCD) or post-traumatic stress disorder (PTSD). In such cases, intrusive thoughts may become entrenched in maladaptive patterns of behavior, triggering compulsive rituals or avoidance strategies aimed at mitigating the perceived threat posed by the intrusive content.

Despite their disruptive nature, intrusive thoughts are not indicative of moral failing or psychological weakness but rather reflect the inherent vulnerability of the human mind to the vagaries of thought and emotion. By acknowledging the presence of intrusive thoughts with compassion and understanding, individuals can begin to cultivate a sense of self-awareness and acceptance, recognizing that these thoughts do not define their identity or determine their worth. Through therapeutic interventions such as cognitive-behavioral therapy (CBT) and mindfulness-based techniques, individuals can develop strategies for managing and coping with intrusive thoughts, reclaiming agency over their mental processes and restoring a sense of equilibrium and resilience to their inner world.

Exploring the common types of intrusive thoughts

Exploring the common types of intrusive thoughts unveils a spectrum of distressing themes that can infiltrate the minds of individuals, regardless of age, gender, or background. One prevalent type revolves around fears of harm, where individuals may be plagued by intrusive thoughts of causing harm to themselves or others, despite lacking any intention or desire to act upon these thoughts. These intrusive thoughts often provoke intense feelings of guilt, shame, and anxiety, leading individuals to question their moral integrity and suitability for social interaction.

Another common subtype of intrusive thoughts centers on themes of contamination or cleanliness, where individuals experience distressing obsessions related to germs, toxins, or bodily fluids. These intrusive thoughts can trigger compulsive behaviors such as excessive handwashing, avoidance of public spaces, or ritualistic cleaning rituals aimed at neutralizing the perceived threat of contamination. Despite their irrationality, these thoughts can exert a powerful hold over individuals, compelling them to engage in repetitive behaviors in an attempt to alleviate their distress.

Additionally, intrusive thoughts may manifest in the form of disturbing or taboo imagery, where individuals experience intrusive mental images or impulses that conflict with their personal values or beliefs. These intrusive thoughts may involve themes of violence, sexuality, or blasphemy, evoking intense feelings of disgust, horror, or shame. Despite efforts to suppress or dismiss these thoughts, they often persist with unwavering intensity, causing considerable distress and disruption to daily functioning.

Furthermore, intrusive thoughts can take the shape of catastrophic or catastrophic scenarios, where individuals experience intrusive fears or worries about potential disasters, accidents, or catastrophic events. These intrusive thoughts may manifest as persistent rumination about worst-case scenarios, leading to heightened anxiety, hypervigilance, and avoidance behaviors aimed at mitigating the perceived threat of harm.

Moreover, intrusive thoughts may also revolve around themes of doubt or uncertainty, where individuals experience intrusive questioning or second-guessing of their own thoughts, decisions, or actions. These intrusive thoughts can undermine one's confidence and self-assurance, leading to feelings of indecisiveness, insecurity, and self-doubt.

In summary, exploring the common types of intrusive thoughts reveals a diverse array of distressing themes that can infiltrate the minds of individuals, causing considerable distress and disruption to daily functioning. From fears of harm and contamination to disturbing imagery and catastrophic scenarios, intrusive thoughts can exert a powerful hold over individuals, triggering intense feelings of guilt, shame, anxiety, and uncertainty. Despite their irrationality, these thoughts persist with unwavering intensity, compelling individuals to engage in compulsive behaviors in an attempt to alleviate their distress. Through understanding and compassionate intervention, individuals can learn to manage and cope with intrusive thoughts, reclaiming agency over their mental processes and restoring a sense of equilibrium and resilience to their inner world.

Recognizing the impact of intrusive thoughts on mental well-being

Recognizing the impact of intrusive thoughts on mental well-being is essential for understanding the profound toll they can exact on individuals' psychological health. Intrusive thoughts have a pervasive influence that extends beyond mere moments of discomfort, often infiltrating various aspects of daily life and undermining overall well-being.

First and foremost, intrusive thoughts can generate intense feelings of distress, anxiety, and fear. Whether they manifest as worries about potential harm, disturbing images, or irrational doubts, these intrusive thoughts can provoke a constant state of unease and hypervigilance. Individuals may find themselves consumed by relentless rumination, unable to escape the grip of their intrusive thoughts, leading to heightened stress levels and a sense of emotional exhaustion.

Furthermore, intrusive thoughts can impair cognitive functioning and decision-making processes. The persistent intrusion of distressing or irrational thoughts can interfere with individuals' ability to concentrate, focus, and make sound judgments. This cognitive impairment can hinder academic or professional performance, strain interpersonal relationships, and diminish overall quality of life.

In addition to the immediate psychological impact, intrusive thoughts can also contribute to the development or exacerbation of mental health conditions such as anxiety disorders, depression, and obsessive-compulsive disorder (OCD). Individuals who experience frequent and distressing intrusive thoughts may be at greater risk for developing these conditions, as the persistent disruption of normal thought processes can disrupt neural pathways and exacerbate underlying vulnerabilities.

Moreover, intrusive thoughts can erode self-esteem and self-confidence, leading individuals to doubt their own competence, integrity, or worthiness. The constant barrage of negative or irrational thoughts can chip away at individuals' sense of self-efficacy and agency, fostering feelings of inadequacy, shame, and self-loathing.

Furthermore, intrusive thoughts can impede social functioning and interpersonal relationships. Individuals may feel compelled to hide or suppress their intrusive thoughts for fear of judgment or rejection, leading to social withdrawal, isolation, and feelings of alienation. Moreover, the distress caused by intrusive thoughts can strain relationships with friends, family members, or romantic partners, as individuals may struggle to communicate their experiences or seek support from others.

Overall, recognizing the impact of intrusive thoughts on mental well-being underscores the importance of addressing these experiences with compassion, understanding, and evidence-based interventions. By acknowledging the profound toll that intrusive thoughts can exact on individuals' psychological health, we can work towards destigmatizing these experiences and fostering a culture of empathy and support for those who struggle with them. Through targeted interventions such as cognitive-behavioral therapy (CBT), mindfulness practices, and medication management, individuals can learn to manage and cope with intrusive thoughts effectively, reclaiming agency over their mental health and restoring a sense of equilibrium and resilience to their lives.

Chapter 2: The Nature of the Human Mind

- Examining the workings of the human mind
- Understanding the mechanisms behind intrusive thoughts
- Discussing the relationship between thoughts, emotions, and behaviors

Examining the workings of the human mind

Delving into the intricate workings of the human mind is a journey of endless fascination, marked by a multitude of engaging questions that beckon exploration. At the forefront of inquiry lies the perennial question: What drives human behavior? Is it the interplay of nature and nurture, or the mysterious workings of the subconscious mind? By unraveling the complexities of human cognition, we seek to uncover the hidden mechanisms that govern our thoughts, emotions, and actions, shedding light on the enigmatic mysteries of the mind.

One of the most intriguing questions in the study of human psychology is: How do memories shape our perception of reality? From cherished childhood memories to traumatic experiences, our past influences the lens through which we view the world. But how do memories form, consolidate, and evolve over time? What role do emotions play in memory formation, and how do memories influence our decision-making processes?

Another captivating question revolves around the nature of consciousness: What is the essence of self-awareness, and how does it emerge from the complex interplay of neural networks? From the subjective experience of being to the elusive phenomenon of the "self," consciousness remains one of the greatest mysteries of the human mind. How do we perceive ourselves and others? What distinguishes conscious awareness from mere perception, and can consciousness be quantified or measured?

Furthermore, the study of emotions raises thought-provoking questions about the nature of affective experience: Why do we experience emotions, and what purpose do they serve in our lives? From the primal instincts of fear and anger to the sublime heights of joy and love, emotions color our existence in vibrant hues. But how do emotions arise, and how do they influence our thoughts, behaviors, and social interactions?

Intriguingly, the phenomenon of decision-making prompts us to ponder the factors that influence our choices: How do we weigh the risks and rewards of different options, and what cognitive processes underlie our decision-making strategies? From intuitive gut feelings to rational deliberation, decision-making encompasses a diverse array of cognitive processes. But how do we navigate the complex terrain of decision-making in an uncertain world, and what role does uncertainty play in shaping our choices?

Moreover, the study of perception raises captivating questions about the nature of sensory experience: How do we make sense of the barrage of sensory information that bombards our senses every moment? From the kaleidoscope of colors that paint our visual world to the symphony of sounds that fill our auditory landscape, perception shapes our understanding of reality. But how do we perceive depth, motion, and form, and how do our perceptual experiences differ from one individual to another?

Additionally, the exploration of intelligence leads us to question the nature of cognitive abilities: What defines intelligence, and how do we measure it? From problem-solving and reasoning to creativity and emotional intelligence, intelligence encompasses a wide range of cognitive faculties. But how do individual differences in intelligence arise, and what factors contribute to cognitive development and decline over the lifespan?

In conclusion, examining the workings of the human mind is an endeavor marked by a plethora of engaging questions that challenge our understanding of what it means to be human. From the mysteries of memory and consciousness to the complexities of emotions and decision-making, the study of psychology invites us to embark on a journey of discovery into the depths of the human psyche. Through inquiry and introspection, we strive to unlock the secrets of the mind, unraveling its enigmatic mysteries one question at a time.

Understanding the mechanisms behind intrusive thoughts

Understanding the mechanisms behind intrusive thoughts delves into the intricate interplay of cognitive processes and neural pathways that give rise to these persistent and distressing experiences. At the core of intrusive thoughts lies the phenomenon of selective attention, wherein certain stimuli capture our focus and dominate our conscious awareness despite our efforts to redirect our attention elsewhere. This selective attention bias predisposes individuals to fixate on threatening or distressing stimuli, amplifying their salience and perpetuating the cycle of intrusive thoughts.

Moreover, the cognitive mechanisms underlying intrusive thoughts often involve maladaptive patterns of thought processing, such as cognitive distortions and rumination. Cognitive distortions, such as catastrophizing, black-and-white thinking, and personalization, distort reality and amplify perceived threats, leading to the generation of intrusive and irrational thoughts. Similarly, rumination involves repetitive and uncontrollable dwelling on distressing thoughts or emotions, fueling the intensity and persistence of intrusive thoughts.

Furthermore, the neural underpinnings of intrusive thoughts implicate a network of brain regions involved in emotion regulation, threat detection, and executive control. Dysfunction within these neural circuits, particularly the prefrontal cortex, amygdala, and anterior cingulate cortex, can disrupt the balance between cognitive control and emotional processing, predisposing individuals to intrusive thoughts and related symptoms. For example, hyperactivity in the amygdala, a key region involved in processing fear and threat, may amplify emotional responses to intrusive thoughts, while deficits in executive control mediated by the prefrontal cortex may impair the ability to suppress or inhibit these thoughts.

Additionally, the role of memory processes in the generation and maintenance of intrusive thoughts is paramount. Memories associated with past traumas or negative experiences may become activated in response to triggering stimuli, leading to the intrusion of distressing thoughts and emotions into conscious awareness. Moreover, memory biases, such as confirmation bias and hindsight bias, can distort the interpretation of incoming information, reinforcing existing beliefs or fears and perpetuating the cycle of intrusive thoughts.

Furthermore, the influence of psychological factors, such as stress, anxiety, and low self-esteem, cannot be understated in understanding the mechanisms behind intrusive thoughts. Heightened levels of stress or anxiety can exacerbate cognitive biases and impair emotion regulation, making individuals more susceptible to intrusive thoughts and related symptoms. Similarly, low self-esteem or negative self-perceptions may amplify feelings of vulnerability and self-doubt, exacerbating the intensity and frequency of intrusive thoughts.

In summary, understanding the mechanisms behind intrusive thoughts involves a multifaceted exploration of cognitive, neural, and psychological processes that contribute to their emergence and persistence. From selective attention biases and cognitive distortions to neural dysregulation and memory processes, a myriad of factors converge to shape the experience of intrusive thoughts. By unraveling these underlying mechanisms, researchers and clinicians can develop targeted interventions aimed at alleviating the burden of intrusive thoughts and promoting mental well-being.

Discussing the relationship between thoughts, emotions, and behaviors

The relationship between thoughts, emotions, and behaviors forms the cornerstone of human experience, shaping our perceptions, actions, and interactions with the world. At its essence, this relationship embodies a dynamic interplay wherein each component influences and is influenced by the others, giving rise to complex patterns of thought, feeling, and action.

Thoughts serve as the cognitive foundation upon which our experiences are constructed. They encompass a broad spectrum of mental processes, ranging from conscious reasoning and problem-solving to automatic thoughts and unconscious biases. Our thoughts can be rational or irrational, positive or negative, constructive or destructive, depending on the underlying beliefs, attitudes, and perceptions that inform them. Importantly, our thoughts not only reflect our internal reality but also play a pivotal role in shaping our emotional responses and behavioral tendencies.

Emotions, in turn, represent the affective dimension of human experience, encompassing a rich tapestry of feelings and sensations that color our subjective experience of the world. Emotions can range from joy and love to anger and fear, each serving as a valuable source of information about our internal state and external environment. Importantly, emotions are closely intertwined with our thoughts, with cognitive appraisals and interpretations often influencing the intensity and valence of our emotional responses. For example, a perceived threat may evoke feelings of fear or anxiety, while a sense of accomplishment may elicit feelings of pride or happiness.

Behaviors, on the other hand, represent the observable manifestations of our thoughts and emotions, encompassing a wide range of actions, responses, and interactions with the world. Our behaviors are guided by a complex interplay of internal and external factors, including our thoughts, emotions, beliefs, values, and environmental context. While some behaviors may be consciously chosen and deliberate, others may be automatic or habitual, reflecting ingrained patterns of thought and emotion that influence our actions without conscious awareness.

The relationship between thoughts, emotions, and behaviors is bidirectional, with each component exerting a reciprocal influence on the others. For example, negative or distorted thoughts can give rise to unpleasant emotions such as sadness, anxiety, or anger, which, in turn, may precipitate maladaptive behaviors such as avoidance, rumination, or aggression. Conversely, engaging in adaptive behaviors, such as problem-solving, relaxation, or social support seeking, can modulate our emotional responses and challenge negative thought patterns, leading to improved psychological well-being.

Importantly, this relationship is not static but dynamic, evolving over time and in response to changing circumstances. Our thoughts, emotions, and behaviors are subject to ongoing processes of appraisal, adaptation, and regulation, influenced by factors such as cognitive flexibility, emotional resilience, and social support. By cultivating awareness of the interconnections between thoughts, emotions, and behaviors, individuals can develop greater insight into their inner experience and enhance their capacity for self-regulation and emotional well-being.

In summary, the relationship between thoughts, emotions, and behaviors forms a complex and dynamic framework that underpins human cognition, emotion, and action. By recognizing the reciprocal influences between these components, individuals can gain a deeper understanding of their thoughts, emotions, and behaviors and cultivate greater self-awareness, resilience, and adaptive coping strategies in the face of life's challenges.

Chapter 3: Introduction to Cognitive Behavioral Therapy (CBT)

- **Explaining the principles of CBT**
- **Understanding how CBT can be applied to manage intrusive thoughts**
- **Discussing the effectiveness of CBT in treating various mental health conditions**

Explaining the principles of CBT

Cognitive Behavioral Therapy (CBT) is a therapeutic approach grounded in the belief that our thoughts, emotions, and behaviors are interconnected and mutually influence each other. At its core, CBT operates on the principle that how we perceive situations and events determines how we feel and behave. By identifying and challenging negative or distorted patterns of thinking, CBT aims to promote more adaptive and constructive ways of coping with life's challenges. Here are some key principles of CBT:

Cognitive Restructuring: One of the central principles of CBT is cognitive restructuring, which involves identifying and challenging irrational or unhelpful thoughts and beliefs. Through techniques such as cognitive reframing and thought challenging, individuals learn to recognize cognitive distortions (e.g., black-and-white thinking, catastrophizing) and replace them with more balanced and realistic perspectives.

Behavioral Activation: Another key principle of CBT is behavioral activation, which focuses on increasing engagement in rewarding and meaningful activities to counteract symptoms of depression or anxiety. By scheduling and gradually reintroducing enjoyable activities into one's routine, individuals can disrupt patterns of avoidance and withdrawal, leading to improved mood and functioning.

Exposure Therapy: In cases where individuals are struggling with anxiety or phobias, exposure therapy may be employed as part of CBT. This technique involves gradually exposing individuals to feared situations or stimuli in a controlled and systematic manner, allowing them to confront and overcome their fears through repeated exposure and habituation.

Skills Training: CBT often includes skills training components aimed at teaching individuals practical coping strategies for managing distressing emotions or challenging situations. These skills may include relaxation techniques, stress management strategies, assertiveness training, and problem-solving skills, among others.

Collaboration and Goal Setting: CBT is a collaborative and goal-oriented approach, with therapists and clients working together to identify treatment goals and develop personalized intervention plans. Through ongoing collaboration and feedback, individuals are empowered to take an active role in their treatment and progress towards their goals.

Psychoeducation: CBT typically involves psychoeducation, where individuals learn about the connection between thoughts, emotions, and behaviors, as well as the principles and techniques of CBT. By gaining a better understanding of the underlying mechanisms of their difficulties, individuals are better equipped to apply CBT strategies in their daily lives.

Homework and Practice: CBT often incorporates homework assignments and practice exercises to reinforce learning and facilitate skill acquisition outside of therapy sessions. These assignments may include keeping thought records, practicing relaxation techniques, or engaging in exposure exercises, allowing individuals to apply CBT principles in real-world situations.

Overall, CBT is a highly structured and evidence-based approach to therapy that emphasizes collaboration, skill-building, and practical application. By targeting maladaptive patterns of thinking and behavior, CBT empowers individuals to develop more adaptive coping strategies, enhance emotional resilience, and improve overall psychological well-being.

Understanding how CBT can be applied to manage intrusive thoughts

Understanding how Cognitive Behavioral Therapy (CBT) can be applied to manage intrusive thoughts offers valuable insights into effective strategies for breaking the cycle of rumination and distress. At the core of CBT lies the principle of cognitive restructuring, which involves identifying and challenging the underlying beliefs and assumptions that give rise to intrusive thoughts. By helping individuals recognize and dispute irrational or distorted thinking patterns, CBT empowers them to develop more balanced and realistic perspectives, reducing the intensity and frequency of intrusive thoughts over time.

One key technique used in CBT to manage intrusive thoughts is cognitive reframing. This involves consciously altering the interpretation of intrusive thoughts by examining evidence for and against them and considering alternative explanations. By reframing negative thoughts in a more neutral or positive light, individuals can reduce their emotional impact and regain a sense of control over their mental processes. For example, instead of catastrophizing about the potential consequences of intrusive thoughts, individuals can challenge these thoughts by considering more realistic and less catastrophic outcomes.

Another important aspect of CBT for managing intrusive thoughts is behavioral activation. This involves engaging in activities that promote a sense of mastery, pleasure, and accomplishment, thereby disrupting the cycle of rumination and avoidance that often accompanies intrusive thoughts. By focusing on valued activities and goals, individuals can redirect their attention away from intrusive thoughts and towards meaningful and fulfilling experiences. Through gradual exposure to triggering stimuli, individuals can also desensitize themselves to the distressing content of intrusive thoughts, reducing their emotional reactivity over time.

Moreover, CBT teaches individuals coping skills to manage the emotional distress associated with intrusive thoughts. These may include relaxation techniques such as deep breathing, progressive muscle relaxation, or mindfulness meditation, which can help individuals regulate their emotions and reduce physiological arousal. By practicing these techniques regularly, individuals can develop greater emotional resilience and tolerance for distress, enabling them to navigate challenging situations with greater calm and composure.

Furthermore, CBT encourages individuals to develop problem-solving skills to address the underlying triggers and contributors to intrusive thoughts. By identifying potential stressors, triggers, or maladaptive coping strategies, individuals can develop practical strategies for managing stress and preventing the escalation of intrusive thoughts. Through collaborative goal-setting and action planning, individuals can take an active role in their treatment and work towards tangible improvements in their mental well-being.

In addition, CBT incorporates elements of mindfulness and acceptance-based approaches to help individuals cultivate present-moment awareness and non-judgmental acceptance of their thoughts and emotions. By learning to observe intrusive thoughts without attaching undue significance or reacting impulsively, individuals can reduce their emotional reactivity and break free from the cycle of rumination and distress. By practicing mindfulness meditation, individuals can develop greater self-awareness and emotional regulation skills, enabling them to respond to intrusive thoughts with greater clarity and equanimity.

Furthermore, CBT often involves psychoeducation about the nature of intrusive thoughts and their relationship to underlying psychological processes. By understanding the cognitive and emotional mechanisms that contribute to intrusive thoughts, individuals can develop greater insight into their experiences and learn to distinguish between intrusive thoughts and reality-based concerns. By normalizing the experience of intrusive thoughts and emphasizing their transient nature, individuals can reduce feelings of shame, guilt, or self-blame, fostering a sense of empowerment and resilience in the face of adversity.

In summary, CBT offers a comprehensive and evidence-based approach to managing intrusive thoughts by addressing the underlying cognitive, emotional, and behavioral processes that contribute to their emergence and persistence. Through techniques such as cognitive reframing, behavioral activation, coping skills training, problem-solving, mindfulness, and psychoeducation, individuals can gain greater insight into their experiences, develop practical strategies for managing distress, and cultivate greater resilience and well-being. CBT provides a roadmap for navigating the challenges posed by intrusive thoughts and reclaiming agency over one's mental health

Discussing the effectiveness of CBT in treating various mental health conditions

Cognitive Behavioral Therapy (CBT) has garnered widespread recognition for its effectiveness in treating a diverse array of mental health conditions. Extensive research and clinical evidence support its efficacy as a first-line treatment for various psychological disorders, ranging from anxiety and depression to obsessive-compulsive disorder (OCD), post-traumatic stress disorder (PTSD), and eating disorders. The versatility and adaptability of CBT make it a valuable therapeutic approach for addressing the underlying cognitive, emotional, and behavioral factors that contribute to these conditions.

In treating anxiety disorders, CBT has proven particularly effective in helping individuals identify and challenge irrational beliefs and distorted thinking patterns that contribute to excessive worry, fear, and avoidance behaviors.

By engaging in exposure-based techniques and behavioral experiments, individuals learn to confront their fears gradually and develop more adaptive coping strategies for managing anxiety symptoms. Research consistently demonstrates significant reductions in anxiety symptoms and improvements in overall functioning following CBT interventions for disorders such as generalized anxiety disorder (GAD), panic disorder, social anxiety disorder, and specific phobias.

Similarly, CBT has demonstrated efficacy in the treatment of depression, offering individuals practical skills and strategies for challenging negative thought patterns, increasing behavioral activation, and enhancing problem-solving abilities. Through cognitive restructuring and behavioral activation techniques, individuals learn to challenge depressive cognitions and engage in pleasurable and meaningful activities that promote mood regulation and emotional well-being. Meta-analytic studies have shown CBT to be as effective as antidepressant medication in reducing symptoms of depression, with enduring effects over time and lower rates of relapse.

CBT is also widely utilized in the treatment of obsessive-compulsive disorder (OCD), a condition characterized by intrusive thoughts and repetitive behaviors or rituals. Through exposure and response prevention (ERP) techniques, individuals with OCD gradually confront feared stimuli or situations and learn to resist engaging in compulsive behaviors, thereby breaking the cycle of obsessions and compulsions. Research has consistently shown ERP, when integrated into a broader CBT framework, to be highly effective in reducing OCD symptoms and improving overall functioning.

Furthermore, CBT has shown promise in the treatment of post-traumatic stress disorder (PTSD), providing individuals with tools for processing traumatic memories, managing distressing symptoms, and rebuilding a sense of safety and control. Through techniques such as trauma-focused cognitive restructuring and exposure therapy, individuals confront and reframe negative beliefs and emotions associated with traumatic events, leading to significant reductions in PTSD symptoms and improvements in quality of life.

In the realm of eating disorders, such as anorexia nervosa, bulimia nervosa, and binge-eating disorder, CBT is considered a cornerstone of treatment, addressing dysfunctional thoughts and behaviors related to body image, food, and weight. By challenging distorted beliefs about body image and addressing maladaptive eating behaviors, individuals learn to develop a healthier relationship with food and body image and cultivate more adaptive coping strategies for managing stress and emotional distress.

In summary, Cognitive Behavioral Therapy (CBT) has demonstrated remarkable effectiveness in treating a wide range of mental health conditions, offering individuals practical skills and strategies for challenging negative thought patterns, managing distressing emotions, and modifying maladaptive behaviors. Through its evidence-based techniques and collaborative approach, CBT empowers individuals to take an active role in their treatment and achieve meaningful improvements in their mental well-being. As such, CBT remains a cornerstone of modern psychotherapy, providing hope and healing to countless individuals struggling with mental health challenges.

Chapter 4: Identifying Negative Self-Talk

- **Recognizing patterns of negative self-talk**
- **Exploring the origins of negative beliefs and attitudes**
- **Learning to challenge and reframe negative self-talk using CBT techniques**

Recognizing patterns of negative self-talk

Recognizing patterns of negative self-talk is a crucial step in cultivating self-awareness and promoting psychological well-being. Negative self-talk refers to the inner dialogue or thoughts characterized by self-criticism, self-doubt, and pessimism, which can undermine self-esteem and contribute to feelings of inadequacy and distress. By identifying common patterns of negative self-talk, individuals can begin to challenge and reframe these unhelpful thought patterns, fostering a more balanced and compassionate self-perception.

One common pattern of negative self-talk is known as "catastrophizing," wherein individuals magnify the perceived negative consequences of a situation and anticipate the worst possible outcome. This pattern of thinking often involves imagining the most dire and exaggerated scenarios, leading to heightened anxiety and distress. For example, someone might catastrophize about a minor mistake at work, believing it will lead to job loss or financial ruin.

Another pattern of negative self-talk is "black-and-white thinking," also known as "all-or-nothing" thinking, wherein individuals view situations in extreme and dichotomous terms, without considering the nuances or complexities involved. This rigid and polarized thinking style can lead to a distorted perception of reality, where individuals perceive themselves or their circumstances as either entirely good or entirely bad. For example, someone might see themselves as a complete failure if they make a small mistake, ignoring their many successes and achievements.

Furthermore, negative self-talk often involves "personalization," wherein individuals attribute blame or responsibility to themselves for events or outcomes that are beyond their control. This pattern of thinking can lead to feelings of guilt, shame, and self-blame, even in situations where they are not warranted. For example, someone might blame themselves for a friend's bad mood, assuming they must have done something to cause it.

Additionally, negative self-talk can manifest as "overgeneralization," wherein individuals draw broad and sweeping conclusions based on isolated incidents or experiences. This pattern of thinking involves extrapolating negative outcomes from specific instances, leading to a pervasive sense of hopelessness or despair. For example, someone might generalize from a single rejection or failure to believe that they are destined to fail in all aspects of their life.

Moreover, negative self-talk often involves "mind reading" or "fortune-telling," wherein individuals make negative assumptions about what others think of them or predict negative outcomes without evidence or justification. This pattern of thinking can lead to social anxiety and avoidance behaviors, as individuals may fear judgment or rejection from others. For example, someone might assume that others find them boring or unlikable, without any concrete evidence to support this belief.

In summary, recognizing patterns of negative self-talk is essential for promoting self-awareness and psychological well-being. By identifying common cognitive distortions such as catastrophizing, black-and-white thinking, personalization, overgeneralization, and mind reading, individuals can begin to challenge and reframe these unhelpful thought patterns, cultivating a more balanced and compassionate self-perception. Through techniques such as cognitive restructuring and mindfulness, individuals can learn to replace negative self-talk with more realistic and positive alternatives, fostering greater resilience and emotional well-being.

Exploring the origins of negative beliefs and attitudes

Exploring the origins of negative beliefs and attitudes unveils a complex interplay of personal experiences, social influences, and cognitive processes that shape our perceptions of ourselves and the world around us. These negative beliefs and attitudes often stem from early childhood experiences, interpersonal relationships, societal messages, and cognitive biases, which can interact in intricate ways to shape our self-concept and worldview.

One significant factor contributing to the development of negative beliefs and attitudes is early childhood experiences, particularly those involving trauma, neglect, or invalidation. Adverse experiences such as abuse, neglect, or parental criticism can leave lasting imprints on individuals' self-esteem and self-worth, leading to the internalization of negative beliefs about themselves and their abilities. For example, a child who grows up in a verbally abusive household may internalize messages of worthlessness or inadequacy, leading to the development of negative self-talk and low self-esteem.

Moreover, interpersonal relationships play a crucial role in shaping individuals' beliefs and attitudes about themselves and others. Negative experiences such as rejection, betrayal, or bullying can reinforce existing insecurities and vulnerabilities, leading individuals to develop negative beliefs about their own worthiness or the trustworthiness of others. Similarly, ongoing conflict or dysfunction within relationships can perpetuate negative patterns of communication and interaction, further reinforcing negative beliefs and attitudes.

Furthermore, societal messages and cultural norms can contribute to the formation of negative beliefs and attitudes, particularly those related to identity, body image, and success. Media portrayals, societal standards, and cultural expectations often promote unrealistic ideals of beauty, success, and happiness, leading individuals to compare themselves unfavorably to these standards and internalize feelings of inadequacy or inferiority. For example, pervasive messages about thinness and beauty in the media can contribute to the development of negative body image and disordered eating behaviors in vulnerable individuals.

Additionally, cognitive biases and distortions play a significant role in shaping individuals' beliefs and attitudes, influencing how they perceive and interpret information about themselves and the world. Cognitive biases such as confirmation bias, selective attention, and overgeneralization can lead individuals to focus on negative information while discounting or ignoring positive experiences, reinforcing negative beliefs and attitudes. For example, someone who experiences rejection in a romantic relationship may selectively attend to instances of rejection while disregarding evidence of acceptance or affection from others.

In summary, exploring the origins of negative beliefs and attitudes reveals a multifaceted interplay of personal experiences, social influences, and cognitive processes that shape our perceptions of ourselves and the world. Early childhood experiences, interpersonal relationships, societal messages, and cognitive biases all contribute to the development and maintenance of negative beliefs and attitudes, which can have profound implications for individuals' self-esteem, mental health, and overall well-being. By gaining insight into the origins of these negative beliefs and attitudes, individuals can begin to challenge and reframe them, fostering greater self-compassion, resilience, and psychological growth.

Learning to challenge and reframe negative self-talk using CBT techniques

Learning to challenge and reframe negative self-talk using Cognitive Behavioral Therapy (CBT) techniques offers individuals practical strategies for cultivating a more balanced and constructive inner dialogue. CBT emphasizes the importance of identifying and challenging irrational or distorted thoughts that contribute to negative emotions and behaviors, empowering individuals to develop more adaptive ways of thinking and responding to challenging situations.

One of the key techniques used in CBT to challenge negative self-talk is cognitive restructuring. This involves systematically identifying and examining the underlying beliefs and assumptions that give rise to negative thoughts, and then evaluating their accuracy and validity. Individuals learn to recognize common cognitive distortions such as catastrophizing, black-and-white thinking, and personalization, and to challenge these distortions by gathering evidence for and against their beliefs. By reframing negative thoughts in a more balanced and realistic light, individuals can reduce their emotional intensity and regain a sense of control over their thoughts and feelings.

Another effective CBT technique for challenging negative self-talk is thought recording or journaling. This involves keeping track of negative thoughts as they arise throughout the day and then systematically analyzing and challenging them using cognitive restructuring techniques. Individuals learn to identify specific triggers or situations that give rise to negative thoughts, as well as the underlying beliefs and assumptions that fuel them. By examining the evidence for and against these beliefs, individuals can develop more balanced and rational responses to challenging situations, leading to a reduction in negative self-talk over time.

Furthermore, CBT teaches individuals to develop alternative or coping thoughts to replace negative self-talk in challenging situations. This involves actively generating more adaptive and constructive responses to negative thoughts, based on evidence and rational analysis. Individuals learn to reframe negative beliefs with more balanced and compassionate statements, such as acknowledging their strengths and accomplishments, recognizing their efforts and progress, or considering alternative explanations for challenging situations. By consciously practicing these coping thoughts, individuals can gradually rewire their neural pathways and cultivate a more positive and resilient mindset.

Additionally, mindfulness techniques are often incorporated into CBT interventions to help individuals cultivate present-moment awareness and non-judgmental acceptance of their thoughts and emotions. By learning to observe negative thoughts without attachment or reactivity, individuals can reduce their emotional intensity and develop greater equanimity in the face of adversity. Mindfulness practices such as meditation, deep breathing, or body scanning can help individuals develop greater self-awareness and emotional regulation skills, enabling them to respond to negative self-talk with greater clarity and calmness.

In summary, learning to challenge and reframe negative self-talk using CBT techniques offers individuals practical and empowering strategies for cultivating a more balanced and constructive inner dialogue. By identifying and challenging irrational or distorted thoughts, keeping track of negative thoughts using thought recording or journaling, developing alternative coping thoughts, and practicing mindfulness techniques, individuals can reduce the intensity and frequency of negative self-talk and foster greater resilience and well-being. CBT provides a roadmap for transforming negative self-talk into a more positive and compassionate self-narrative, empowering individuals to take control of their thoughts and emotions and lead more fulfilling lives.

Chapter 5: Understanding Cognitive Distortions

- **Defining cognitive distortions**
- **Identifying common cognitive distortions associated with intrusive thoughts**
- **Learning strategies to counter cognitive distortions through CBT**

Defining cognitive distortions

Cognitive distortions are patterns of biased or irrational thinking that can lead individuals to perceive reality inaccurately or negatively. These distortions often involve systematic errors in reasoning or interpretation, leading individuals to misinterpret information, overgeneralize, or make illogical conclusions about themselves, others, or the world around them. Cognitive distortions are a hallmark feature of various psychological disorders, including depression, anxiety, and obsessive-compulsive disorder (OCD), and can contribute to the maintenance of emotional distress and maladaptive behaviors.

One common cognitive distortion is catastrophizing, wherein individuals exaggerate the perceived negative consequences of a situation and anticipate the worst possible outcome. This pattern of thinking often involves imagining catastrophic scenarios or worst-case scenarios that are unlikely to occur in reality. For example, someone might catastrophize about failing a test, believing it will lead to academic failure, unemployment, and financial ruin.

Another cognitive distortion is black-and-white thinking, also known as all-or-nothing thinking, wherein individuals view situations in extreme and dichotomous terms, without considering the nuances or complexities involved. This rigid and polarized thinking style can lead individuals to see things in terms of absolutes, such as success or failure, good or bad, right or wrong. For example, someone might view themselves as a complete failure if they make a minor mistake, ignoring their many successes and accomplishments.

Furthermore, cognitive distortions often involve overgeneralization, wherein individuals draw broad and sweeping conclusions based on isolated incidents or experiences. This pattern of thinking involves extrapolating negative outcomes from specific instances, leading to a pervasive sense of hopelessness or despair. For example, someone might generalize from a single rejection or failure to believe that they are destined to fail in all aspects of their life.

Additionally, cognitive distortions can manifest as personalization, wherein individuals attribute blame or responsibility to themselves for events or outcomes that are beyond their control. This pattern of thinking can lead to feelings of guilt, shame, and self-blame, even in situations where they are not warranted. For example, someone might blame themselves for a friend's bad mood, assuming they must have done something to cause it.

Moreover, cognitive distortions often involve selective attention, wherein individuals focus selectively on negative information while discounting or ignoring positive experiences. This pattern of thinking can lead individuals to overlook evidence that contradicts their negative beliefs or assumptions, reinforcing their distorted perception of reality. For example, someone might dwell on a single criticism or rejection while disregarding numerous instances of praise or acceptance from others.

In summary, cognitive distortions are patterns of biased or irrational thinking that can lead individuals to perceive reality inaccurately or negatively. These distortions often involve catastrophizing, black-and-white thinking, overgeneralization, personalization, and selective attention, among others, and can contribute to emotional distress and maladaptive behaviors. By recognizing and challenging these cognitive distortions, individuals can develop more balanced and realistic ways of thinking, leading to improved emotional well-being and functioning.

Identifying common cognitive distortions associated with intrusive thoughts

Identifying common cognitive distortions associated with intrusive thoughts can offer valuable insight into the underlying thought patterns that contribute to their persistence and distress. Intrusive thoughts often trigger cognitive distortions that amplify their intensity and make them seem more threatening or meaningful than they truly are. By recognizing these distortions, individuals can begin to challenge and reframe their intrusive thoughts, reducing their emotional impact and breaking the cycle of rumination and distress.

One common cognitive distortion associated with intrusive thoughts is catastrophizing, wherein individuals exaggerate the perceived negative consequences of their thoughts and anticipate the worst possible outcomes. For example, someone experiencing intrusive thoughts about harming a loved one might catastrophize about losing control and causing irreversible harm, even though the likelihood of such an event occurring is extremely low.

Another cognitive distortion commonly associated with intrusive thoughts is black-and-white thinking, also known as all-or-nothing thinking, wherein individuals view their thoughts in extreme and dichotomous terms, without considering the nuances or complexities involved. This rigid and polarized thinking style can lead individuals to see their thoughts as either entirely good or entirely bad, without recognizing shades of gray or alternative perspectives. For example, someone might view themselves as inherently flawed or dangerous because of their intrusive thoughts, ignoring evidence to the contrary.

Furthermore, intrusive thoughts often trigger overgeneralization, wherein individuals draw broad and sweeping conclusions based on isolated instances or experiences. This pattern of thinking involves extrapolating negative outcomes from specific thoughts, leading to a pervasive sense of hopelessness or despair. For example, someone experiencing intrusive thoughts about contamination might overgeneralize these thoughts to believe that they are dirty or contaminated in all aspects of their life.

Additionally, intrusive thoughts can lead to personalization, wherein individuals attribute excessive blame or responsibility to themselves for their thoughts or their consequences. This pattern of thinking can lead to feelings of guilt, shame, and self-blame, even when individuals have no control over the content or frequency of their intrusive thoughts. For example, someone might blame themselves for having intrusive thoughts about harming others, assuming they must be a bad person for having such thoughts.

Moreover, intrusive thoughts often trigger selective attention, wherein individuals focus selectively on the negative aspects of their thoughts while discounting or ignoring positive experiences or evidence to the contrary. This pattern of thinking can reinforce the perceived significance or threat of intrusive thoughts, making them seem more pervasive or meaningful than they truly are. For example, someone might dwell on a single intrusive thought about harming a loved one while disregarding the countless instances of care and affection they have shown towards that person.

In summary, identifying common cognitive distortions associated with intrusive thoughts can help individuals gain insight into the underlying thought patterns that contribute to their distress and persistence. By recognizing patterns of catastrophizing, black-and-white thinking, overgeneralization, personalization, and selective attention, individuals can begin to challenge and reframe their intrusive thoughts, reducing their emotional impact and fostering greater resilience and well-being. Cognitive-behavioral techniques such as cognitive restructuring and mindfulness can be particularly helpful in addressing these cognitive distortions and promoting more adaptive ways of thinking.

Learning strategies to counter cognitive distortions through CBT

Individuals may learn to confront and reframe negative thinking patterns via Cognitive Behavioral Therapy (CBT), which helps them develop a more balanced and constructive attitude by teaching them techniques to fight cognitive distortions. Individuals may learn to think and react more adaptively to difficult circumstances via cognitive behavioral therapy (CBT), which provides a range of evidence-based approaches for recognizing and correcting cognitive distortions.

Cognitive restructuring is a powerful tool in cognitive behavioral therapy (CBT) for overcoming cognitive distortions. This method entails looking for illogical or distorted ideas and then methodically arguing against them by analyzing the arguments for and against them. Cognitive distortions like overgeneralization, catastrophizing, and black-and-white thinking are ubiquitous, but people may learn to recognize and combat them via guided inquiry and Socratic questioning. One way to lessen the impact of negative ideas and get back control of one's thoughts is to reframe them in a more reasonable and objective perspective.

Behavioral experiments are another tactic used in cognitive behavioral therapy to combat cognitive biases. Here, one uses empirical methods like observation and experimentation to see if preconceived notions about a problem are correct. Individuals may collect data to counter their negative beliefs and confirm their predictions by planning and carrying out behavioral studies. If you think you're unlikable, you may try talking to a new person and seeing how they react; this would provide you data to dispute your negative self-perception.

Furthermore, CBT enables people to generate alternate or coping beliefs to replace negative self-talk and cognitive distortions. This entails intentionally producing more adaptable and constructive reactions to negative beliefs, based on data and reasonable analysis. Individuals learn to reframe negative ideas with more balanced and compassionate comments, such as appreciating their strengths and successes, recognizing their efforts and growth, or contemplating alternate reasons for hard events. By intentionally practicing these coping concepts, people may progressively rewire their brain connections and create a more optimistic and resilient mentality.

Additionally, mindfulness practices are commonly included into CBT therapies to assist clients acquire present-moment awareness and non-judgmental acceptance of their thoughts and feelings. By learning to notice unpleasant ideas without attachment or response, people may lower their emotional intensity and achieve more equanimity in the face of hardship. Mindfulness activities such as meditation, deep breathing, or body scanning may help people acquire more self-awareness and emotional regulation abilities, allowing them to react to cognitive distortions with greater clarity and tranquility.

In essence, learning skills to fight cognitive distortions via Cognitive Behavioral Therapy (CBT) provides people practical and powerful tools for confronting and reframing their negative thinking patterns. By participating in cognitive restructuring, behavioral experiments, establishing alternative coping beliefs, and practicing mindfulness, people may lower the severity and frequency of cognitive distortions and create a more balanced and productive mentality. CBT offers a comprehensive framework for altering negative thought patterns and developing increased resilience and well-being.

Chapter 6: Overcoming Obsessive-Compulsive Disorder (OCD)

- **Understanding the nature of OCD**
- **Exploring the role of intrusive thoughts in OCD**
- **Introducing CBT techniques specifically tailored for managing OCD symptoms**

Understanding the nature of OCD

Obsessive-Compulsive Disorder (OCD) is a psychiatric condition characterized by the presence of obsessions and compulsions that significantly interfere with daily functioning and cause distress. Understanding the nature of OCD requires a nuanced appreciation of its complex and multifaceted features, encompassing both cognitive and behavioral components.

Obsessions are intrusive and persistent thoughts, urges, or images that are experienced as distressing and unwanted, leading to feelings of anxiety or discomfort. Common obsessions in OCD may revolve around themes such as contamination, symmetry, orderliness, or harm, and individuals often engage in compulsive behaviors or rituals in an attempt to alleviate their distress.

People who suffer from obsessions or who behave rigidly in reaction to certain thoughts or feelings may engage in compulsive actions in an effort to alleviate their anxiety or avoid a negative consequence. Some compulsions might be more obvious than others; for example, compulsive hand washing, checking, or counting. Others, like mental counting or praying, are more subtle. Compulsions, while offering short-term comfort, have a tendency to reinforce the obsessional and anxious cycles, which in turn perpetuate the dysfunctional and distressing patterns associated with Obsessive-Compulsive Disorder (OCD).

Anxiety and dysfunction in many areas of functioning, such as social, occupational, and intellectual ones, characterize obsessive-compulsive disorder (OCD). The bothersome and time-consuming nature of compulsions and obsessions may greatly impact the everyday lives of people with obsessive-compulsive disorder. Because obsessive-compulsive disorder symptoms may take up a lot of energy and time, people with OCD may find it difficult to maintain relationships, keep a job, or pursue academic pursuits.

Furthermore, the nature of OCD is defined by a chronic and variable course, with symptoms waxing and waning over time in response to numerous stresses and triggers. While some people may have periods of remission or partial recovery, OCD tends to be a chronic and lifelong disorder for many individuals. Without adequate treatment and support, the symptoms of OCD may have a dramatic influence on persons' quality of life, leading to feelings of despair, humiliation, and isolation.

Understanding the nature of OCD also includes identifying the underlying neurological and genetic elements that contribute to its development and manifestation. Research shows that anomalies in brain circuitry, especially affecting regions such as the orbitofrontal cortex, anterior cingulate cortex, and basal ganglia, may have a role in the pathogenesis of OCD. Additionally, genetic factors are likely to contribute to sensitivity to OCD, with evidence showing a family aggregation of the condition and heritability estimates ranging from 40% to 65%.

Moreover, the nature of OCD comprises a varied presentation, with people experiencing a broad variety of symptom profiles and severity levels. While some people may appear with mostly obsessional symptoms, others may display primarily compulsive symptoms, and yet, others may have a mix of both. The particular content and form of obsessions and compulsions may vary greatly across people, reflecting the many ways in which OCD can appear across different individuals and cultural situations.

In essence, understanding the nature of OCD needs a full grasp of its clinical symptoms, course, neurological basis, and heterogeneity. Obsessions and compulsions lay at the core of OCD, leading to severe suffering and impairment in numerous domains of functioning. By comprehending the intricate interaction of cognitive, behavioral, and neurobiological aspects involved in OCD, clinicians and people alike may create more effective ways for evaluation, treatment, and management of this debilitating condition.

Exploring the role of intrusive thoughts in OCD

Delving into the function of intrusive thoughts in Obsessive-Compulsive Disorder (OCD) is like exploring a labyrinth laden with shadows and uncertainty. Intrusive thoughts, analogous to unwelcome visitors crashing a party, create havoc in the brains of persons dealing with OCD. These ideas, like unrelenting opponents hammering at the door of sanity, interrupt the calm of people' mental landscapes, leaving them caught in a cycle of worry and compulsion.

At the center of OCD lies the delicate dance of obsessions and compulsions, comparable to a devil's bargain where one feeds off the other. Obsessions, like obstinate echoes resonating in the hallways of the mind, torment people with painful and nonsensical content. These beliefs, whether concentrated on contamination concerns, worry of harm befalling loved ones, or the desire for symmetry and order, hold great influence over people' thoughts and behaviors, leaving them feeling helpless in their aftermath.

Compulsions, like frantic efforts at warding off bad spirits, occur when people seek sanctuary from the continuous attack of obsessions. These recurrent activities or mental routines, analogous to a sailor grabbing to a sinking ship's mast, give short solace from the anguish inside. Yet, like a mirage in the desert, compulsions bring only short solace, driving patients further into the labyrinth of OCD's grasp.

The function of intrusive thoughts in OCD resembles a puppeteer controlling marionettes with exquisite precision, commanding people' thoughts and behaviors with an iron grasp. These ideas, like rough waves threatening to capsize a boat, steal folks' attention and destroy their feeling of control. The invasive nature of these ideas strips people of their individuality, leaving them adrift in a sea of uncertainty, anxiously seeking safe harbor.

Moreover, the importance of intrusive thoughts in OCD goes beyond ordinary mental occurrences, spreading a lengthy shadow over persons' lives like a gloomy cloud on a beautiful day. Relationships, employment, and leisure activities become battlegrounds where people fight war against the continuous assault of obsessions and compulsions. The pervasive nature of intrusive thoughts leaves folks feeling alienated, embarrassed, and desperate for relief, like a lone wanderer wandering in the woods with no compass to guide them.

In conclusion, investigating the function of intrusive thoughts in OCD uncovers the dark underbelly of this devastating condition. Obsessions, like thunderclouds hovering on the horizon, threaten to unleash a storm of pain and sorrow. Compulsions give brief refuge from the storm, but eventually drive folks further into the labyrinth of OCD's grips. By comprehending the tremendous influence of intrusive thoughts on patients' lives, physicians and individuals alike may chart a route towards calmer seas, bringing hope for a better future among the shadows of uncertainty.

Introducing CBT techniques specifically tailored for managing OCD symptoms

Introducing Cognitive Behavioral Therapy (CBT) approaches particularly adapted for controlling Obsessive-Compulsive Disorder (OCD) symptoms provides patients practical options for breaking free from the hold of obsessions and compulsions. CBT for OCD emphasizes a planned and methodical approach aimed at questioning and altering the underlying cognitive patterns and behaviors that contribute to the cycle of misery and dysfunction typical of the illness. By learning and practicing these approaches, people may restore a feeling of control over their thoughts and actions, lower the severity and frequency of symptoms, and enhance their overall quality of life.

One essential CBT strategy for controlling OCD symptoms is exposure and response prevention (ERP). ERP includes consistently exposing patients to events, objects, or ideas that trigger their obsessions while preventing them from participating in obsessive actions or routines. Through frequent exposure to feared stimuli and extended exposure to anxiety-provoking events, people learn to accept and habituate to their obsessions, diminishing the anxiety and discomfort associated with them over time. By severing the connection between obsessions and compulsions, ERP helps patients build more adaptive coping methods for controlling their symptoms.

Another CBT strategy for controlling OCD symptoms is cognitive restructuring. Cognitive restructuring entails recognizing and confronting unreasonable or distorted beliefs related with obsessions and compulsions, and replacing them with more balanced and realistic alternatives. Individuals learn to detect typical cognitive distortions such as catastrophizing, black-and-white thinking, and overgeneralization, and to question these distortions by accumulating evidence for and against their ideas. By reframing unfavorable ideas in a more objective and reasonable perspective, people may lower their emotional intensity and restore a feeling of control over their thoughts and actions.

Additionally, CBT for OCD generally combines behavioral experiments and cognitive rehearsal methods to help patients verify the validity of their ideas and assumptions, and build more adaptive ways of reacting to their obsessions and compulsions. Behavioral studies entail methodically testing predictions or hypotheses about feared consequences or beliefs via real-world experiences, so giving participants with actual data to question their erroneous thinking habits. Cognitive rehearsal strategies entail mentally practicing more adaptive reactions to frightening circumstances or ideas, helping people build better confidence and self-efficacy in controlling their symptoms.

Moreover, mindfulness-based approaches are increasingly being included into CBT therapies for OCD to assist patients acquire present-moment awareness and non-judgmental acceptance of their thoughts and feelings. By learning to observe their obsessions and compulsions without attachment or response, people may lower their emotional intensity and achieve more serenity in the face of uncertainty. Mindfulness activities such as meditation, deep breathing, or body scanning may help patients develop higher self-awareness and emotional regulation abilities, helping them to react to their symptoms with greater clarity and tranquility.

In summary, adopting CBT approaches particularly suited for controlling OCD symptoms provides clients practical and powerful solutions for breaking free from the hold of obsessions and compulsions. Through treatments like exposure and response prevention, cognitive restructuring, behavioral experiments, and mindfulness-based techniques, people may build more adaptive coping skills for controlling their symptoms and reclaiming their life from the tyranny of OCD. CBT offers a blueprint for conquering the hurdles faced by

OCD, bringing hope and healing to those dealing with this debilitating condition.

Chapter 7: Managing Toxic Thoughts

- **Recognizing toxic thoughts and their impact on mental health**
- **Learning strategies to identify and challenge toxic thoughts using CBT**
- **Exploring mindfulness techniques to promote mental clarity and emotional resilience**

Recognizing toxic thoughts and their impact on mental health

Toxic thoughts and their effects on mental health must be acknowledged in order to support resilience and emotional well-being. Negative or harmful thought patterns that exacerbate emotions of misery, inadequacy, and despair are referred to as toxic thoughts. These ideas may manifest in a variety of ways, including self-criticism, rumination, catastrophizing, and self-doubt. They often do so in reaction to difficult circumstances or ingrained ideas about oneself and the outside world.

One prevalent kind of harmful thinking is negative self-talk, in which people speak to themselves constantly, criticizing and doubting themselves. This kind of thinking may undermine confidence and self-worth, resulting in depressing and hopeless sentiments. Harsh and condemning language said to oneself is a common component of negative self-talk, which serves to reinforce emotions of worthlessness and inadequacy.

Toxic ideas may also take the form of rumination, a condition in which people can't let go of unpleasant feelings or experiences and instead keep thinking about the past or their perceived shortcomings. This kind of thinking may feed emotions of regret, worry, and melancholy, creating a vicious cycle of emotional suffering and rumination. Rumination often entails mentally reliving unpleasant situations or occurrences and exaggerating their importance and effects on one's life.

Additionally, catastrophizing—the act of exaggerating the perceived negative effects of a situation and projecting the worst possible outcome—is often associated with poisonous thinking. This kind of thinking may exacerbate anxiety and panic, making people feel powerless and overwhelmed in the face of hardship. When someone is catastrophizing, they often imagine worst-case scenarios or catastrophic events without taking into account more realistic or balanced viewpoints.

Furthermore, negative thinking may manifest as self-doubt, in which people doubt their value, worth, or ability. This kind of thinking may erode motivation and self-worth, making it difficult to pursue objectives or take steps toward constructive change. When someone has self-doubt, they often downplay their successes and virtues in favor of concentrating on their alleged flaws or failings.

Furthermore, negative thinking patterns may exacerbate emotions of shame and guilt, which lead people to hold themselves accountable for perceived inadequacies or errors. It might be challenging to forgive oneself and move on when one has a persistent feeling of unworthiness and self-loathing due to this thought pattern. An emotional roller coaster of self-blame and internalized ideas about one's own shortcomings or deficiencies is often the cause of shame and guilt.

To sum up, encouraging self-awareness and emotional well-being requires an understanding of toxic beliefs and how they affect mental health. Individuals may start the process of challenging and reframing harmful thought patterns, such as negative self-talk, rumination, catastrophizing, self-doubt, shame, and guilt, by recognizing typical negative thought patterns. This can help to cultivate a more positive and compassionate internal dialogue. People may develop a more robust and balanced attitude by practicing strategies like cognitive restructuring, mindfulness, and self-compassion. This will enable them to face life's obstacles with more clarity and fortitude.

Learning strategies to identify and challenge toxic thoughts using CBT

Learning strategies to identify and challenge toxic thoughts using Cognitive Behavioral Therapy (CBT) offers individuals practical tools for promoting mental well-being and resilience. CBT techniques focus on increasing awareness of negative thinking patterns and developing more adaptive ways of responding to them, thereby reducing emotional distress and improving overall functioning. By learning and applying these strategies, individuals can gain greater control over their thoughts and emotions, leading to greater self-confidence and improved quality of life.

Cognitive restructuring is a crucial CBT technique for recognizing and disputing harmful ideas. Cognitive restructuring is the process of methodically recognizing, assessing, and substituting more realistic and balanced ideas with negative or distorted ones. People get knowledge about typical cognitive distortions, such overgeneralization, black-and-white thinking, and catastrophizing, and how to confront them by assembling evidence both in favor of and against their opinions. People might lessen their emotional intensity and recover control over their thoughts and emotions by rephrasing unfavorable ideas in a more objective and reasonable way.

Thought monitoring, often known as journaling, is another method used in CBT to recognize and confront harmful ideas. This entails monitoring negative ideas as they come to mind throughout the day, and cognitive restructuring tools to analyze and challenge them methodically. People get the ability to recognize the particular circumstances or triggers that result in poisonous ideas, as well as the underlying presumptions and beliefs that support them. People may learn to respond to difficult circumstances in a more balanced and logical way by weighing the facts for and against their negative ideas. This can eventually reduce their emotional pain.

Furthermore, CBT teaches people how to create coping mechanisms or alternate beliefs to replace harmful ones under difficult circumstances. This entails deliberately coming up with more sensible and helpful replies, supported by logic and facts, to negative beliefs. People learn how to counteract negative ideas with more compassionate and reasonable comments, such praising their efforts and growth, recognizing their successes, or exploring other options for explaining difficult circumstances. Through deliberate use of these coping strategies, people may progressively remodel their brain circuits and develop a more optimistic and robust mentality.

Furthermore, CBT therapies often include mindfulness-based strategies to support clients in developing present-moment awareness and accepting their thoughts and feelings without passing judgment. Through the practice of seeing poisonous ideas objectively and without connection or reaction, people may lessen the intensity of their emotions and become more composed when faced with challenges. Individuals may react to poisonous ideas more calmly and clearly by practicing mindfulness techniques like deep breathing, body scanning, and meditation. These techniques can also help people become more self-aware and adept at regulating their emotions.

In conclusion, developing CBT skills to recognize and confront harmful beliefs gives people useful and powerful tools to support resilience and mental health. By using strategies like cognitive restructuring, thought monitoring, creating coping ideas, and mindfulness, people may learn more adaptive methods to deal with their negative thought patterns, which will lessen their emotional discomfort and enhance their general functioning. Cognitive Behavioral Therapy (CBT) offers a path for changing negative thinking patterns into a more healthy and productive internal dialogue, enabling people to take charge of their ideas and feelings and live happier, more satisfying lives.

Exploring mindfulness techniques to promote mental clarity and emotional resilience

People may develop more self-awareness and composure in the face of life's obstacles by studying mindfulness practices that enhance mental clarity and emotional resilience. The practice of mindfulness, which has its roots in antiquated contemplative traditions, entails being open, curious, and accepting of the present moment. People may improve their general well-being, mental clarity, and emotional resilience by practicing mindfulness.

Practicing mindfulness meditation, which involves focusing attention on the breath, physical sensations, or other anchor points, helps people develop present-moment awareness. People may train their brains to become more focused and attentive, which will lessen the inclination to dwell on the past or worry about the future, by gently guiding their attention back to the present whenever it wanders. It has been shown that practicing mindfulness meditation may increase emotional resilience, ease stress, and improve mental clarity in general.

Body scan meditation is another mindfulness practice in which practitioners methodically focus on various body areas, observing sensations without interpretation or judgment. People may strengthen their feeling of connection to their physical self and become more aware of the present moment by learning to cultivate awareness of their body sensations. People may develop a stronger feeling of relaxation and well-being, let go of stress, and experience less physical pain by practicing body scan meditation.

Furthermore, to encourage increased self-awareness and stress reduction, mindfulness-based stress reduction, or MBSR, is a structured program that combines body scan meditation, mindfulness meditation, and moderate yoga poses. Dr. Jon Kabat-Zinn created Mindfulness-Based Stress Reduction

(MBSR), which has been extensively studied and shown to be beneficial in lowering symptoms of anxiety, depression, and chronic pain as well as enhancing general quality of life. People may increase their emotional resilience and coping mechanisms by practicing mindfulness on a regular basis. This will help them react to life's obstacles with more clarity and composure.

Furthermore, to assist people in escaping negative thought patterns and rumination, mindfulness-based cognitive therapy (MBCT) integrates mindfulness techniques with the concepts of cognitive behavioral therapy (CBT). People may increase their cognitive flexibility and emotional management abilities and lower their chance of relapsing into depression or anxiety by learning to notice their thoughts objectively and without attachment or reaction. For those with a history of recurrent depression, MBCT has been shown to be useful in avoiding relapse, providing an important means of fostering long-term emotional resilience.

In addition, informal mindfulness techniques include attention into routine tasks like walking, eating, and dishwashing. People may concentrate better, feel less stressed, and have better general health by practicing present-moment mindfulness in their everyday lives. Informal mindfulness practices may be especially helpful for fostering mental clarity and emotional resilience in the face of everyday problems. They also provide a useful and approachable means of incorporating mindfulness into hectic schedules.

In conclusion, using mindfulness practices to strengthen mental acuity and emotional fortitude provides people with a strong route to increased contentment and well-being. People can improve their overall quality of life, self-awareness, and emotional resilience by practicing present-moment awareness through techniques like body scan meditation, mindfulness meditation, mindfulness-based stress reduction, mindfulness-based cognitive therapy, and informal mindfulness practices. A timeless knowledge that comes from mindfulness enables people to handle life's ups and downs with more compassion, clarity, and peace of mind.

Chapter 8: Practicing Mindfulness and Self-Compassion

- **Introducing mindfulness as a tool for managing intrusive thoughts**
- **Cultivating self-compassion to counteract self-criticism and judgment**
- **Incorporating mindfulness and self-compassion practices into daily life**

Introducing mindfulness as a tool for managing intrusive thoughts

People may reclaim control of their brains and lessen the anguish brought on by unwanted ideas by using mindfulness as a practical and powerful method for handling intrusive thoughts. The practice of mindfulness, which has its roots in antiquated contemplative traditions, entails being open, curious, and accepting of the present moment. Through practicing mindfulness, people may become more aware of their thoughts and feelings and learn how to react to them calmly and clearly.

Acquiring the ability to perceive intrusive thoughts objectively and without bias is a fundamental component of mindfulness. People might just observe their ideas as fleeting mental phenomena, like clouds moving across the sky, rather than becoming engrossed in their meaning or substance. People may lessen the emotional intensity and anguish that come with intrusive thoughts by taking a non-reactive approach to them, which promotes acceptance and inner peace.

Additionally, mindfulness exercises like body scan and mindfulness meditation may aid in the development of better mental clarity and concentration, which will facilitate the disengagement from distracting ideas and the redirection of attention to the present moment. People who regularly practice mindfulness may teach their brains to become more flexible and robust, which will eventually loosen the hold that intrusive ideas have over them.

Furthermore, to assist people in escaping negative thought patterns and rumination, mindfulness-based cognitive therapy (MBCT) integrates mindfulness techniques with the concepts of cognitive behavioral therapy (CBT). Through practicing mindfulness meditation, people may improve their cognitive flexibility and emotional control, which will lessen the frequency and severity of intrusive thoughts. MBCT is a useful strategy for controlling intrusive thoughts and has been shown to be successful in lowering symptoms of anxiety, sadness, and obsessive-compulsive disorder (OCD).

In addition, informal mindfulness techniques include attention into routine tasks like walking, eating, and dishwashing. People may lessen their propensity to dwell on the past or worry about the future by practicing present-moment awareness on a regular basis. This will make it simpler to stop worrying about unimportant things and concentrate on what is important right now.

In conclusion, teaching mindfulness as a strategy for controlling intrusive thoughts gives people a comprehensive and empowered approach to mental health. Through practicing mindfulness, people may become more aware of their thoughts and feelings, learn how to react to them calmly and clearly, and lessen the suffering brought on by unpleasant ideas. By releasing people from the hold of intrusive thoughts, mindfulness provides a timeless knowledge that enables people to take back control of their brains and lead more fulfilled lives.

Cultivating self-compassion to counteract self-criticism and judgment

Cultivating self-compassion offers a powerful antidote to the self-criticism and judgment that often accompany intrusive thoughts and negative thinking patterns. Self-compassion involves treating oneself with kindness, understanding, and acceptance, especially in times of difficulty or suffering. By cultivating self-compassion, individuals can counteract the harsh inner critic and develop a more supportive and nurturing relationship with themselves.

One key aspect of self-compassion is recognizing that suffering and imperfection are part of the human experience. Rather than viewing oneself as flawed or inadequate for experiencing intrusive thoughts or negative emotions, individuals can acknowledge their humanity and offer themselves the same kindness and understanding they would offer to a friend in similar circumstances. By embracing their own imperfections with self-compassion, individuals can reduce the tendency towards self-criticism and judgment, fostering greater emotional resilience and well-being.

Moreover, self-compassion involves practicing self-kindness and self-care in the face of difficulty or distress. Rather than berating oneself for perceived failures or shortcomings, individuals can offer themselves words of comfort and encouragement, as they would to a loved one in need. This may involve practicing self-soothing techniques such as deep breathing, mindfulness, or engaging in activities that bring joy and comfort. By nurturing themselves with self-compassion, individuals can soothe the pain of intrusive thoughts and negative emotions, fostering a sense of inner peace and acceptance.

Additionally, self-compassion involves adopting a mindful and non-judgmental stance towards one's thoughts and feelings. Rather than getting caught up in the content or meaning of intrusive thoughts, individuals can observe them with curiosity and acceptance, recognizing that thoughts are transient mental events that do not define their worth or identity. By approaching intrusive thoughts with mindfulness and self-compassion, individuals can reduce their emotional intensity and disengage from the cycle of self-criticism and rumination.

Furthermore, self-compassion involves recognizing the common humanity in our struggles and failures. Rather than feeling isolated or ashamed for experiencing intrusive thoughts or negative emotions, individuals can recognize that suffering is a universal human experience and that they are not alone in their struggles. By embracing their shared humanity with self-compassion, individuals can reduce feelings of shame and isolation, fostering a sense of connection and belonging with others.

In summary, cultivating self-compassion offers a powerful antidote to self-criticism and judgment, especially in the face of intrusive thoughts and negative thinking patterns. By treating oneself with kindness, understanding, and acceptance, individuals can counteract the harsh inner critic and develop greater emotional resilience and well-being. Through practices such as recognizing common humanity, offering self-kindness, practicing mindfulness, and nurturing oneself with self-care, individuals can cultivate a more compassionate relationship with themselves, freeing themselves from the grip of self-criticism and judgment, and fostering greater peace and acceptance in their lives.

Incorporating mindfulness and self-compassion practices into daily life

Incorporating mindfulness and self-compassion practices into daily life offers individuals a practical and transformative way to cultivate greater well-being, resilience, and inner peace. These practices can be integrated seamlessly into everyday activities, helping individuals to navigate life's challenges with greater clarity, kindness, and acceptance.

One simple way to incorporate mindfulness into daily life is through mindfulness meditation. This involves setting aside a few minutes each day to sit quietly and focus on the present moment, paying attention to the sensations of the breath or other anchor points. By practicing mindfulness meditation regularly, individuals can develop greater mental clarity and emotional resilience, making it easier to respond to stressors with calmness and equanimity.

Another way to integrate mindfulness into daily life is through informal mindfulness practices. This involves bringing mindful awareness to everyday activities such as eating, walking, or washing dishes. By paying attention to the sensations, sights, sounds, and smells of the present moment, individuals can cultivate greater presence and appreciation for the simple joys of life. Informal mindfulness practices offer opportunities to pause and savor the richness of each moment, reducing the tendency to rush through life on autopilot.

Moreover, incorporating self-compassion practices into daily life can help individuals cultivate greater kindness, understanding, and acceptance towards themselves and others. One way to practice self-compassion is through self-kindness exercises, such as offering oneself words of comfort and encouragement in times of difficulty or distress. By treating oneself with the same kindness and compassion one would offer to a friend in need, individuals can soothe the pain of self-criticism and judgment, fostering greater emotional resilience and well-being.

Additionally, practicing mindfulness and self-compassion in interpersonal interactions can deepen connections with others and foster a sense of empathy and compassion towards oneself and others. By listening attentively, being fully present, and responding with kindness and understanding, individuals can cultivate more meaningful and authentic relationships, enhancing their sense of connection and belonging.

Furthermore, setting aside time each day for reflection and self-care can help individuals recharge and replenish their emotional reserves, making it easier to cope with life's challenges. This may involve engaging in activities that bring joy and relaxation, such as spending time in nature, pursuing hobbies, or practicing self-care rituals like taking a warm bath or reading a favorite book. By prioritizing self-care and nurturing oneself with kindness and compassion, individuals can maintain a sense of balance and well-being amidst the busyness of daily life.

In summary, incorporating mindfulness and self-compassion practices into daily life offers individuals a pathway to greater well-being, resilience, and inner peace. By integrating mindfulness meditation, informal mindfulness practices, self-compassion exercises, and self-care rituals into daily routines, individuals can cultivate greater presence, kindness, and acceptance in their lives, fostering greater emotional resilience and well-being. Through regular practice and commitment, individuals can transform their relationship with themselves and others, leading to a more fulfilling and meaningful life.

Chapter 9: Sustaining Progress and Moving Forward

- **Reflecting on the journey of overcoming intrusive thoughts**
- **Developing strategies to maintain progress and prevent relapse**
- **Setting goals for continued personal growth and well-being**

Reflecting on the journey of overcoming intrusive thoughts

It is a very personal and transforming experience to reflect on the road of conquering intrusive thoughts; it is replete with times of difficulty, development, and perseverance. As people face their innermost fears and phobias and learn to bravely and compassionately traverse the stormy seas of their own thoughts, it is a voyage of self-discovery and inner healing.

At the beginning of the voyage, people might experience an overwhelming and helpless sense in the face of their own thoughts as they get trapped in a never-ending maelstrom of intrusive ideas. Realizing that these ideas are fleeting mental occurrences that come and go like clouds in the sky rather than defining who they are is the first step in the trip. Reaching this awareness marks the beginning of the process of healing and regaining control over one's own thoughts and feelings.

People learn to practice mindfulness as they go along the path, opening up to the present moment with acceptance, curiosity, and openness. People who engage in mindfulness exercises, like meditation, become more aware of their thoughts and feelings and learn how to react to them calmly and clearly. They learn that they don't have to be prisoners to their ideas and that they can choose how they interact with them.

People also learn how to develop self-compassion, which is the ability to be kind, understanding, and accepting of themselves—especially during trying or painful situations. They learn to use gentle self-care to ease the pain of self-criticism and judgment, and they give themselves words of consolation and encouragement, just as they would to a friend in need. People who practice self-compassion find a renewed feeling of inner peace and acceptance as well as increased emotional resilience and wellbeing.

People have setbacks and hurdles along the way, as well as times of dread, uncertainty, and doubt. However, every obstacle presents a chance for development and education as people face their anxieties head-on and come out stronger and more resilient than before. They discover how to develop bravery in the face of misfortune and how to have faith in their own natural ability to heal and evolve.

In the end, conquering intrusive thoughts is a constant process of development rather than a straight line. It is a path of self-awareness and empowerment as people learn to compassionately and wisely negotiate the complexity of their own brains. They go from the darkness of their own ideas into the light of self-awareness and acceptance with every stride they take ahead, gaining more clarity, resilience, and inner peace.

Developing strategies to maintain progress and prevent relapse

Sustaining long-term resilience and well-being requires developing methods to keep up the gains and avoid relapsing when it comes to beating intrusive thoughts. Although the road to rehabilitation may include ups and downs, having a proactive strategy in place may support people in staying on course and overcoming obstacles. Here are some tactics to think about:

Consistent Practice: To strengthen healthy routines and develop emotional resilience, practice self-compassion and mindfulness on a regular basis. Even in periods of relative stability, try to implement these habits into your daily routine since consistency is important.

Determine Triggers: Keep an eye out for circumstances, ideas, or feelings that often lead to intrusive thoughts. Understanding your triggers can help you create better coping mechanisms and keep things from getting out of control and leading to a complete relapse.

Create a Toolkit of Coping Mechanisms: Assemble a set of mechanisms to handle stress, worry, and other emotions that might intensify intrusive thoughts. This might include gradual muscular relaxation, guided meditation, deep breathing techniques, or indulging in enjoyable activities that enhance wellbeing and relaxation.

Challenge Cognitive Distortions: Using cognitive behavioral strategies, keep up the fight against cognitive distortions and negative thought patterns. Reframe negative beliefs and create more realistic, balanced viewpoints by engaging in cognitive restructuring exercises.

Remain Socially Involved: Seek out assistance from loved ones, friends, or support groups. Talking about your experiences with like-minded people may provide support, encouragement, and useful guidance on how to deal with intrusive thoughts.

Self-Care: Make self-care a priority and partake in activities that enhance mental, emotional, and physical health. This might include exercising often, maintaining a healthy diet, getting adequate rest, and scheduling leisure and pastime time.

Track Your Progress: Celebrate all of your accomplishments, no matter how little, and keep a record of your progress over time. Consider the progress you've made and the abilities you've acquired to deal with intrusive thoughts. Make use of this reflection as inspiration to keep going.

Seek expert Assistance: Do not be afraid to see a therapist or other mental health expert if intrusive thoughts start to seriously interfere with your everyday functioning or if they become overpowering. Therapy, in particular mindfulness-based techniques or cognitive behavioral therapy (CBT), might provide more assistance and direction in controlling intrusive thoughts and averting relapse.

Make a Relapse Prevention strategy: Work with your mental health professional or therapist to create a relapse prevention strategy. This plan should include specific warning indicators, coping mechanisms, and actions to take in the event that you experience relapse symptoms. Planning beforehand will enable you to react swiftly and efficiently in the event that intrusive thoughts reappear.

You may continue to make improvements and develop resilience over time by implementing these techniques into your everyday activities and continuing to take proactive measures to deal with intrusive thoughts. Recall that getting well is a journey, and obstacles are normal along the way. Remain dedicated to your well-being, have self-compassion, and be gentle with yourself.

Setting goals for continued personal growth and well-being

Establishing objectives for ongoing wellbeing and personal development is crucial to sustaining advancement and leading a happy existence. These objectives may relate to any number of facets of life, such as one's physical, mental, social, and spiritual health. The following are some suggestions for goal-setting to encourage continuous development and wellbeing:

Physical Health Objectives: Establish objectives for your physical well-being, such as regular exercise, a balanced diet, enough sleep, and routine medical check-ups. Try adding some of your favorite activities—like yoga, swimming, or jogging—to your schedule on a regular basis.

Emotional Well-Being Objectives: Pay attention to objectives that enhance emotional resilience and well-being, such as developing healthy relationships, handling stress properly, and engaging in self-compassion and mindfulness exercises. Think about scheduling time each day for relaxation and joy-filled activities such as writing or meditation.

Goals for Social Connections: Give special attention to establishing and maintaining relationships with friends, family, and the community. Make time for the people you love, make an effort to meet new people, and join clubs or activities that share your beliefs and interests.

Personal Development Goals: Establish goals for your own personal development, such as picking up new skills, pursuing interests or hobbies, or taking on significant challenges. Think about enrolling in courses, going to seminars, or looking for mentors who can help you grow and develop.

Career and Educational Goals: Establish objectives for your work and education, such as moving up the corporate ladder in your present role, going back to school or getting training, or looking into alternative professional paths. Make a schedule for accomplishing these objectives and break them down into manageable chunks.

Financial Goals: Make changes to your financial situation by establishing objectives for debt repayment, investing, saving, and budgeting. To establish a financial plan that is in accordance with your objectives and long-term goals, think about collaborating with a financial counselor or making use of internet resources.

Spiritual or Personal Growth Objectives: Contemplate your principles, convictions, and sense of direction, then establish objectives that bolster your spiritual or personal development path. This may be taking up new spiritual pursuits, volunteering or giving back to the community, or taking part in soul-nourishing activities that strengthen your connection with something bigger than yourself.

Setting objectives to give importance to things that feed and revitalize your mind, body, and soul can help you make self-care a priority. Setting limits, declining engagements or activities that deplete your energy, and scheduling downtime for hobbies, leisure, and introspection are a few examples of how to do this.

Setting SMART (specific, measurable, attainable, relevant, and time-bound) objectives is crucial for ongoing personal development and wellbeing. Divide more ambitious objectives into manageable chunks, then acknowledge and acknowledge your accomplishments as you go. Be adaptable and prepared to change course as necessary to take into account new priorities or circumstances. You may design a life that is purposeful, well-rounded, and consistent with your beliefs and ambitions by establishing meaningful goals and making a commitment to continuous development and self-improvement.

Conclusion: Embracing Mental Freedom

- **Encouraging readers to continue applying CBT techniques to achieve mental freedom**
- **Inspiring hope and resilience in the journey toward overcoming intrusive thoughts**

Encouraging readers to continue applying CBT techniques to achieve mental freedom

It is important to emphasize the transformational potential of Cognitive Behavioral Therapy (CBT) procedures and to inspire trust in their effectiveness in order to encourage readers to continue using CBT approaches for mental emancipation. With the help of CBT, people may manage troubling emotions, question harmful thinking patterns, and develop better habits, all of which contribute to improved psychological health and resilience. Readers may be motivated to keep using CBT methods by highlighting the following points:

First of all, it's important to emphasize that CBT is widely beneficial in treating a variety of mental health issues and that it is supported by data. The topic is grounded on clinical evidence and empirical research, giving readers confidence in the validity and reliability of CBT procedures. Emphasizing testimonies and success stories might help readers believe even more in the transformational power of CBT.

Second, while readers work with CBT approaches, urge them to have an open and curious mentality. Stress that obstacles are unavoidable and that development is a lengthy process. Readers may overcome obstacles with resiliency and drive by cultivating a mindset of patience and self-compassion. Remind them that any progress, no matter how little, is a triumph to be cherished.

Thirdly, provide helpful advice on how to incorporate CBT methods into regular life. Urge readers to schedule specific time for completing cognitive restructuring activities, practicing mindfulness, and putting behavioral methods into practice. To make routines or activities more accessible and long-lasting, propose integrating these strategies into them. Readers may gain resilience and mental freedom in the long run by incorporating CBT into their daily life.

In the fourth section, emphasize how crucial self-awareness and self-monitoring are to the CBT process. Urge readers to watch, without passing judgment, their feelings, thoughts, and actions, noting any patterns or triggers that add to their suffering. Gaining more self-awareness helps readers pinpoint their areas of improvement and customize their CBT regimen to fit their own requirements and situation.

Fifth, emphasize to readers how ideas, feelings, and actions are intertwined and how modifications in one area may have an impact on other areas. Urge them to try out various CBT methods and approaches to see which ones suit them the best. Highlight how CBT empowers people by putting them in control of their own mental health path.

Sixth, provide readers who may be having difficulties or setbacks with their CBT practice help and encouragement. Reassure them by telling them that getting treatment from a therapist or other mental health expert is a show of strength rather than weakness. Reiterate that no matter how tiny a step is, it still moves them closer to their objectives and that development is not linear.

Seventh, encourage a feeling of solidarity and community among readers by telling tales of tenacity and resilience. Draw attention to the common humanity found in the battles and victories over intrusive thoughts and destructive thought patterns. Urge readers to use social media, internet forums, or support groups to get in touch with others who are traveling similar paths.

Finally, encourage readers to picture the life and person they want to lead, free from the mental and intrusive limits that hold them back. Urge them to develop a vision of resilience and mental freedom and to pursue it with bravery and unflinching resolve. Remind readers that they are in control of their own fate and that they may use CBT to accomplish long-lasting change if they are persistent and dedicated to the process.

Inspiring hope and resilience in the journey toward overcoming intrusive thoughts

Inspiring hope and resilience in the journey toward overcoming intrusive thoughts is a beacon of light amidst the darkness of mental turmoil. It is a reminder that despite the challenges we face, there is always the potential for growth, healing, and transformation. By fostering hope and resilience, individuals can navigate the ups and downs of their journey with courage and determination, knowing that they possess the inner strength to overcome adversity and emerge stronger on the other side.

One of the most powerful ways to inspire hope and resilience is by sharing stories of triumph over adversity. Hearing about others who have successfully overcome intrusive thoughts and reclaimed their lives can instill a sense of possibility and optimism in those who are struggling. These stories serve as reminders that no matter how difficult things may seem, there is always hope for a brighter future.

Additionally, providing practical tools and strategies for building resilience can empower individuals to face their challenges with confidence and determination. This may include techniques such as mindfulness meditation, cognitive restructuring, and self-compassion practices, which have been shown to enhance resilience and promote mental well-being. By equipping individuals with these tools, they can develop the inner resources needed to navigate the twists and turns of their journey with grace and resilience.

Encouraging individuals to cultivate a mindset of growth and self-compassion is another important aspect of inspiring hope and resilience. Remind them that setbacks and obstacles are a natural part of the journey, and that they should treat themselves with kindness and understanding during difficult times. By embracing a growth mindset, individuals can view challenges as opportunities for learning and growth, rather than insurmountable obstacles.

Furthermore, fostering a sense of connection and community can provide invaluable support and encouragement along the journey toward overcoming intrusive thoughts. Encourage individuals to reach out to friends, family, or support groups for guidance and support. Knowing that they are not alone in their struggles can provide a sense of comfort and solidarity, and remind them that there are others who understand and empathize with what they are going through.

Lastly, remind individuals that healing is a journey, not a destination, and that progress may come in small, incremental steps. Encourage them to celebrate their victories, no matter how small, and to acknowledge the progress they have made along the way. By focusing on the positive aspects of their journey and celebrating their resilience and courage, individuals can stay motivated and inspired to continue moving forward, even in the face of adversity.

In summary, inspiring hope and resilience in the journey toward overcoming intrusive thoughts is a powerful act of compassion and support. By sharing stories of triumph, providing practical tools and strategies, fostering a growth mindset, fostering a sense of connection and community, and celebrating progress, individuals can navigate their journey with courage, determination, and resilience, knowing that they have the inner strength to overcome whatever challenges may come their way.

www.ingramcontent.com/pod-product-compliance
Lightning Source LLC
Chambersburg PA
CBHW061048250726
48653CB00001B/306